+

A BARKLEY BOOK

COPYRIGHT © 2021 BARKLEY, INC.
All rights reserved.
All trademarks are the property of their respective companies.
Design and illustrations by Barkley Design & Experience.
Cataloging-in-Publication Data is on file with the Library of Congress.
ISBN: 978-0-578-88152-2
Proudly Printed in the USA

THE MEDIA ADVANTAGE

How to Reframe Marketing
For a World Gone Dark

Jim Elms

FOREWORD

FOREWORD

Media is
an idea

FOREWORD

TIM GALLES

CHIEF IDEA OFFICER,
BARKLEY

Despite what Jim says, we did not meet at Keens Steakhouse in Manhattan, but that's the way he likes to remember the story. I chalk it up to his love of context and ideas. Keens makes the story a lot more interesting and memorable. The real story goes back a few years and begins amidst a different kind of context.

(rewind to me in college, long before I meet Jim)

It's the first day of a class that's been billed by my fellow students as one of the best creative advertising classes in the country, taught by one of the best instructors in the biz. The instructor asks us to bring in an example of an ad we think is great.

"Simple," I think: I'm a student of advertising, this is easy. The great creative thinker and original crazy ad man, George Lois, comes to mind. He's just done an ad for Pauline Trigere, intended to generate some press for the iconic fashion designer who's been missing the coverage she'd earned from W Magazine in her earlier days. Bad boy Lois comes up with an idea of simply running an open letter penned to John Fairchild, then-publisher and editor-in-chief of W and Women's Wear Daily. It's in Ms. Trigere's letterhead and handwriting. The ad runs one time only in the Sunday Magazine of The

New York Times, a once-a-week media event that everyone in fashion reads. As Mr. Lois is famous for saying, creativity can solve almost any problem, and this is one of those ideas that does just that. I love it because it is more than an ad. It's an event, a cannon shot aimed directly at one person. It's an idea that can only happen amidst powerful context. I rush out to get the Sunday Times just so I can clip this ad and take it into class. Surely my professor will think it's brilliant.

He does not.

"If it takes you that long to explain it," he says, "there's no way it can be a good ad." He is forceful and slightly angry: "Find me a clever headline and a clever visual. That's a good ad."

I drop the class immediately. I've never been both so sure and unsure of myself, but I know in my heart that he's both an ass and wrong — and if he's right, I want nothing to do with the kind of formulaic work he celebrates and teaches. I want to pursue a different approach that reads something like this:

```
+ + + + + + + + + + + + + + + + + + + + + + + + + + + +
+                                                      +
+   Media  is  an  idea,  and  contextual  thinking  is   +
+   as  important  as  words  and  pictures,  sometimes   +
+   even more.                                          +
+                                                      +
+ + + + + + + + + + + + + + + + + + + + + + + + + + + +
```

Anyone in marketing or brand work who is not passionate and studious about context does not understand how people behave and live and are missing a giant piece of the creative puzzle.

From this day forward, I will be on an elusive hunt for other people who believe what I believe and think about ideas and the power of them. I have no idea what a tough search it will be, how, more often than not, my media partners will be more interested in carpet bombing with GRPs and TRPs and efficiencies than they'll be in ideas. I'll be surprised to find how many will be okay sitting and waiting to hear from their creative brethren to come up with ideas and then get to work planning where to stick those ideas. I will grow practiced in pleading until I'm blue in the face: "No, no ... you, too, can have ideas. Media can and should be part of the solution. Get upstream. Fight to get in the room. You have the keys to the kingdom, you own the budgets and you should know how people behave."

(fast forward through the commercials to 2011:
my first meeting with Jim Elms)

Jim's reputation for creativity has preceded him. He is a legend at the agency where I work, having left a few years earlier to lead media during the creative renaissance at Grey in New York. In his wake, he left an agency that was more open-minded and creative. People still talk of Jim Elms in hushed tones, as if his creative ghost still walks the hallways and stairwells. I find myself wondering: Who is this guy?

I know I'm going to like Jim because everyone says he is one of the most creative and strategic people they have ever known. Not once do they mention that he runs the media department. In fact, he had been offered the role I eventually take at Barkley — Chief Idea Officer — not because he is great at media but because he is a great creative and strategic generalist.

I did like him. And in the years to come, I frequently call Jim out of the blue to talk ideas and creativity, sometimes veering into discussions about media, but mostly, it is all about ideas. We share references, books, videos and even the nerdiest thing on earth, Keynote decks. To us, this makes sense and is normal. In mere minutes, Jim shares something he is into and I am inspired. The Elms halo lasts me for weeks.

And when, on a trip to see Jim in Manhattan, he shows me a presentation he and his team prepared for Unilever, answering the brief: what do we do in a world without paid advertising, what he calls a World Gone Dark, I know we have to find a way to work together. This brief is eerily consistent with my brain's quest to figure out how Barkley, a siloed creative company, can not only redefine a brand as every action a company or organization takes, but also invite such brands into a new way of seeing opportunity — through whole brand thinking. Such a mindset fuels what happens when brands use creativity across a wide spectrum of actions, not just marketing.

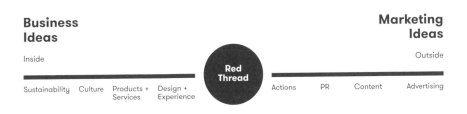

Alas, I've found a co-conspirator, collaborator, partner in crime who is willing to challenge the status quo of our industry. Jim is a creative generalist who happens to be a media expert. A unicorn. The Holy Grail. And someone I talk about ideas, upstream, not downstream only at execution and distribution time. Because the best ideas not only create their own media plan, they create their own media. They are talked about and shared like wild fire.

From this point on, Jim helps me truly think of brands as living in a World Gone Dark, a world where ideas have to work even harder to connect with people because paid advertising is becoming more and more challenged.

Jim helps me really understand and be even more devoted to the philosophy that media and contextual thinking should be as much a part of the creative process as strategy, writing, art direction and design.

(now we are here, to you and this book)

Media as an idea is not a radical or provocative statement or a flag in the ground. This has always been the case. The best thinkers and the best brands have always known it. But those are mostly few and far between.

Jim and I have had some great adventures since our first meeting. One of my favorites was traveling to Tokyo with Jim to help with one of his famous "table sessions." There I am, with Jim's initiation and partnership, leading a team of global Amazon executives and a global IPG creative team in a workshop to imagine Amazon's opportunity for the Tokyo Olympics. This is only the kind of project Jim could be at the center of.

Jim and I still love to discuss media as an idea, often over a Japanese Whisky. Jim has come as close as anyone I've ever met to defining methods to achieve this, and this book will absolutely help you do this. We haven't cracked this huge opportunity yet, the one that involves infusing media with creativity and context, and we need more people to think like Jim, beyond flow charts, media mixes and regression analysis (whatever the hell that is).

Media is the key to the kingdom. It is where the money is spent. Why has it never been a hotbed of creativity? This has been one of the headscratchers of my career.

I truly hope this important book you are holding in your hands brings as much attention as possible to the idea of media as a creative tool and unfair advantage.

May it help everyone that is tasked with bringing brands and their ideas to life, that media and the context in which it presents has to be as much a part of the idea as direction, design systems and overall strategy. And may it inspire more people to take up the torch of media as a powerful creative tool and unfair advantage.

We don't need more art directors, designers and writers. But we desperately need masters and mistresses of context. The second media takes a back seat or is an afterthought, a flare should go off. It means you are headed for an idea that no one sees, cares about or participates with, an idea that is neither modern nor takes advantage of the powerful media landscape. By reframing your view of the value media can provide, you will not only unlock tremendous financial gains but also develop whole brand actions that will modernize your relationship with your customers and communities.

Thank you to Johannes Gutenberg, Guglielmo Marconi, Philo Farnsworth and Tim Berners-Lee for creating the technology, contexts and environments that continue to shape our world. And, thank you to Jim for writing this powerful book and respecting the thinking that came before and is yet to come. Like your management style, you drop timely inspiration, opening our minds to what can and should be.

Kanpai!

"As a life-long student of human nature, Jim offers all of us the opportunity to build better brands. He's a media pioneer who will not only have you rethinking how you approach your media strategy but how you define it."

David Rosenberg, Amazon Global Marketing

"Jim Elms has somehow crammed 30 years of keen observation into a few dozen pages of business-changing insights. Whether you want to change your world or change THE world, this book is your anthem."

Pio Schunker, Executive Vice President, Global CMO, Samsung

CONTENTS

+

CONTENTS

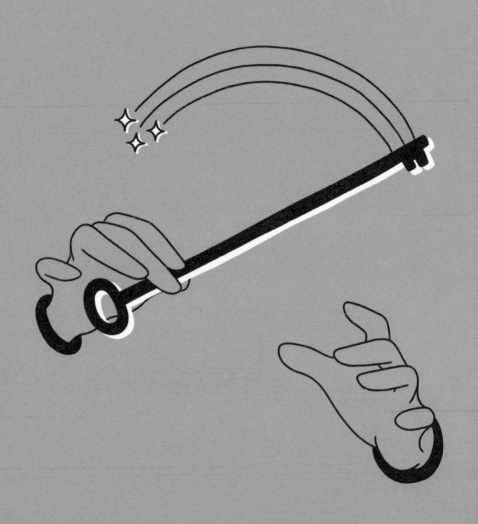

INTRODUCTION

"Turn and face
the strange
changes."

You are holding a book, one of the oldest forms of "media." Thank you, Mr. Gutenberg.

Unfortunately, most business books are out of date the moment they are printed. Thank you apps, blogs, newsletters, alerts, podcasts. Word of mouth.

You are already an expert in media, it's literally in your face 24/7 — x2 to account for multitasking. Every single day, you are exposed to thousands of media ideas that should drive your imagination. Unfortunately, this does not happen enough.

Because the media practice is unnecessarily complicated.

Because the media practice is fogged with acronyms and jargons and sometimes less than well-intentioned behaviors.

Because most media practitioners are forced to live in a box of small expectations.

Media is the most underrated asset in your marketing budget.

The intent of this book is not to inform you about today's news in the media space, or ten tips on challenger brands, or five mega trends in media. You can find hundreds of relevant resources for that on your phone at this very moment.

Rather, think of this book as a set of keys. Each chapter contains an idea, or experience or model that will help you extract more value from your media expenditures.

Chapter One explores a concept called a World Gone Dark: What would your brand do if paid media no longer existed? You'll see a model to develop ideas that will push your media investments to new heights.

Chapter Two challenges the role of the media deliverable: How can you or your teams squeeze every ounce of value from your media budget by reimagining the multiple layers of ideas that your media can deliver?

Chapter Three inspires clear articulation of the linear expectations of your media plan. Turning a flywheel model into a modern media funnel creates vast efficiencies on talent, speed, team synergies and ultimately, whole brand performance.

Chapter Four focuses on systems. Learn to manage your workflow in a way that is laser-quick responsive and combines agility with relevance by positioning media insights at the center of your whole brand management.

Chapter Five is full of modern ideas, methods and inspiration on a personal level. How do you reframe your perspective to drive ideas that turn into word of mouth?

—

Your media budget is likely the largest line-item budget expenditure within your control. If this book can fire one tiny spark in your imagination as you consider a new way to leverage such an investment, reading this book may be the highest ROI activity of your year.

And while the world brings strange change by the minute, impacting the way we consume, avoid and reimagine media, my hope is that this book helps evolve your own thinking, for however long it remains relevant.

Dear Jim,

I always go for the Big Idea. A creative thinker must be fearless. You can be cautious or you can be creative — but there's no such thing as a cautious creative. A great creative idea should bring tears to your eyes, unhinge your nervous system — knock you out.

All great creativity should communicate in a nanosecond . . . Teamwork might work in building an Amish barn, but it can't create a Big Idea. Everybody believes in co-creativity. Not me. Be confident in your own edgy, solo talent.

That's what I think and believe, every second I live and work.

Sincerely,
George Lois

ONE

On a World Gone Dark, the tiger's cave + elegant questions

"The advertising industry has a problem: People hate ads."

New York Times, October 28, 2019

"Nobody reads ads. People read what interests them. Sometimes, it's an ad."

Howard Gossage

It was a mid-November afternoon in 2015 when Leah Meranus burst into my work space with an email from our largest client, Unilever. A global brand with a solid gold reputation.

"Look at this."

In her hands was a note from our client Rob Master, written in prose, describing an almost science-fiction-like future of media that he called a World Gone Dark. In this version of reality, paid media disappeared — no TV ads, no billboards, no banners.

While a modern consumer might call this utopia, for the second-largest media-spending corporation in the world, with a reported global spend of over $7 billion, it's a nightmare. Add to our anxiety the fact that Luis diComo has created one of the most progressive and creative media teams in the world, and you can start to get a sense of the beautiful anxiety Leah and I were feeling.

The timing was tight, our response was due in six weeks, and the ask was straightforward:

What should a brand do in a world with no paid advertising?

It was a powerful brief on many levels, bold yet quite appropriate to ask the three global agency powerhouses this question: "What is the future of media?" It centered on our very own survival.

Our first thought, quite obviously, was that if paid media went away, my company's entire business went with it. Simply put, no paid media, no media agency necessary to plan and buy it. No media planners. No media buyers. No me.

That was a sobering moment.

It was also the most inspirational moment in my career. It required me to consider disrupting ourselves — and myself — before we fell victim to changing business models. It pushed me to rethink our core business propositions: our purpose, products, talent, compensation. Everything we did needed to be reassessed.

As a human, a World Gone Dark is quite a beautiful place, since by its very nature, it rids the world of unwanted interruptions. But as a marketer, the challenges of marketing become even more enormous.

"It's harder to reach audiences, the cost of marketing is going up, the number of channels has exponentially proliferated and the cost to cover all of those channels has proliferated," Jay Pattisall, a lead analyst for Forrester, told the New York Times[1] in a piece on advertising's existential crisis. "It's a continual pressure for marketers — we're no longer just creating advertising campaigns three or four times a year and running them across a few networks and print."

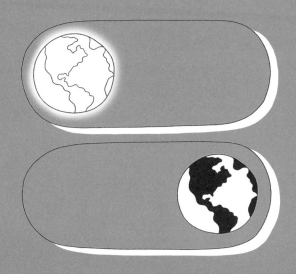

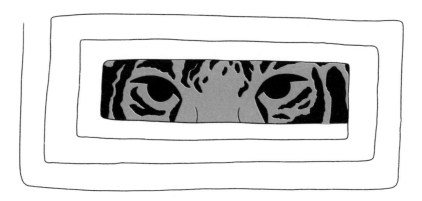

Entering the tiger's cave

The Japanese have a famous saying, "If you do not enter the tiger's cave, you will not catch its cub." The meaning is similar to our American version, "no risk, no reward."

Let's borrow the metaphor and apply it to your brand: the tiger's cave is a place to reframe everything you have learned about creating successful brands. Modern brands are not just a logo or marketing message — it's every action your company or organization takes, from the inside out — a philosophy that's key for evolving into a brand built for the future, one that can thrive in a world without paid advertising.

"Good stories are the true currency
in the world. Great ideas create
their own media."

Tim Galles, Chief Idea Officer, Barkley

In his book "Scratch: How to build a potent modern brand from the inside out," author Tim Galles dedicates an entire chapter to discovering ways into the tiger's cave, to creating brave, bold actions that "are not ad ideas, but ideas worth advertising." These ideas, when done right, he says, create their own media in the form of PR, vital word of mouth and contagious social sharing.

But let's get back to a World Gone Dark. With no paid media, no paid content, there are less obvious places for brands to engage/interrupt. This forces brands to lead with actions Galles refers to in his book — ways to build genuine engagement with consumers who prefer good stories over fabricated messages to fuel the advertising industrial complex.

Tiger's cave actions that paid off big

VOLVO — Created glow-in-the-dark paint for bicycles.

STATE STREET GLOBAL ADVISORS — Installed a statue of an empowered girl in front of the iconic Wall Street Bull to urge more than 3,500 companies to diversify their governing boards.

PANTONE® — Created a boutique hotel.

LE LABO® — Publishes a regular newspaper dedicated to words overheard in its stores.

A modern brand has a meaningful role in the world

Behind the unique actions of Tiger's Cave brands, all have something in common: a purpose that fuels why the brand exists to begin with. Yes, brand purpose is an overused and sometimes under-appreciated term in marketing. In today's world, it's often little more than a press piece for charitable giving. But designed with purpose (haha), it can be an extremely powerful way to connect with consumers.

In "The Purpose Advantage: How to unlock new ways of doing business," entrepreneur and speaker Jeff Fromm says purpose must first be foundational: "It's a clearly defined and long-term strategy that affects every part of the business, from innovation to product development to consumer experience to marketing. It connects with consumers' values and passions, attracting and retaining high-quality talent, spurring creativity and driving growth. Purpose doesn't stop at the mission statement; it influences every decision at every level."

If your brand doesn't have a purpose, start with this simple exercise. Consider your brand as a hero. All heroes need a purpose. What problem, need or opportunity can you solve, fulfill or embrace for the consumers you're trying to reach? How can you inspire your customers' lives?

Your answer can be as simple and broad as you need it to be. Having purpose will lead you to a genuine meaning for existence, and will absolutely inspire ideas and identify new ways of considering utility.

```
+ + + + + + + + + + + + + + + + + + + + + + + + + + +
+                                                   +
+   Your brand's purpose must matter. (duh) Give    +
+   it meaning.                                      +
+                                                   +
+ + + + + + + + + + + + + + + + + + + + + + + + + + +
```

If purpose is your why, meaning is your what: what you communicate, demonstrate, illustrate and share. This is how you prove what your entire brand believes in, actively lives and plays out in every action at every level, from custodians to the C-suite.

But be careful. Communities are quick to investigate the truth behind what you say and what you do.

```
+ + + + + + + + + + + + + + + + + + + + + + + + + + + + + + +
+                                                           +
+    Utility requires explaining what your                  +
+    meaning means.                                         +
+                                                           +
+ + + + + + + + + + + + + + + + + + + + + + + + + + + + + + +
```

When your audience purchases your product or service, how do they really benefit? How are you useful, profitable, beneficial to your customers?

Within economics, the concept of utility is used to model worth or value. Its usage has evolved significantly over time. The term was introduced initially as a measure of pleasure or satisfaction within the theory of utilitarianism by moral philosophers such as Jeremy Bentham and John Stuart Mill. The term has been adapted and reapplied as a utility function that represents a consumer's preference ordering over a choice set. Utility has thus become a more abstract concept that is not necessarily solely based on the satisfaction or pleasure received.[2]

Purpose ⟶ Meaning ⟶ Utility

How does this lead to tangible ideas in a modern world?

Once you have purpose with meaning, the fun begins. How can you use that to leverage ideas that are useful to the consumers you serve? It's time to begin exploring opportunities, exposures, consideration and interactions. Think about all the places your brand plays. Some key territories include:

Rethink the Role of Retail
How do your customers want to buy from you today and tomorrow?

Identify a New Brand Utility
How can your brand create additional value through packaging, distribution or usage?

Curate Culture in a Genuine Way
How can your brand legitimately use content to enhance your customers' lives?

Embrace Your Competition
How can you partner with your competitors to create a better world through technology, design, services, operations?

Be a Force For Good
What are the ways and means you can use your total brand assets to create good for your customers, communities and the world?

These questions provide a useful space to explore opportunities like technology, social habits and message delivery. Additionally, layering in ideas from emerging technologies and high-value customer segments can cement your cultural connections. Obviously, your industry and business will drive these considerations, and depending on your brand distribution and your customer decision pathway, the connection opportunities are customized for each brand.

Brand actions for a World Gone Dark

Turned its product into a movie.

Tim Cook stood up for personal privacy with a well-timed speech in response to Facebook's full-page ads.

Created the #optoutside campaign to encourage its employees and customers to spend Black Friday outside with their families instead of shopping.

From energy drink to media company.

Shared a video to Barbie's official YouTube channel where she and a friend discuss racism and privilege.

After identifying and prioritizing non-paid media brand territories, it's time to design an operational framework to inspire and build ideas. From an organization perspective, your framework should be something that is easily understood by everyone in your entire company, from your CEO to an entry-level hire.

Four steps to building a World Gone Dark model

one	A narrative description of the idea. A 60-second elevator pitch describing the general idea. Name it.
two	Examples of brands living or moving into that idea space to bring the concept to life and to illustrate how the idea could grow beyond. Look outside your category.
three	Three models to guide how the idea might live and be evaluated within the organization, using constructs that align with your industry model and constraints.
four	Examples of actual creative implementations and executions to bring the concept to life.

Let's go back and take the Rethink the Role of Retail as an example.

---

step one   **Develop a narrative description of the general idea.**
This is a building block, your rally cry, your fight song, your flag. It should consider unmet consumer (human) needs and describes a landscape where the brand can tackle the consumer opportunity with a commercial lens. It also describes the opportunity within the intersection of your interactions. Consider it an internal manifesto for ideas.

"You, like many others, have been held captive by retailers. In a world gone dark, there's an opportunity to take back that control — to set yourself free from the restrictions, demands and fees, and inevitably bypass the confining rules of brick-and-mortar retail.

We call this: 'Bite the Hand.'

Traditional retail models are being turned on their heads, and your biggest competitors are no longer your category rivals; price wars, e-comm, deep trade discounts, incentives, vouchers, direct-to-consumer (DTC), free economy and ever-increasing choices are eating away at your shelf space. And it doesn't stop there.

For your customers, things have changed too. Shopping at their leisure, 24 hours a day/365 days a year, has become the norm. Ordering a favorite product happens at the touch of a button — from home, work, a plane, or even from a park bench. And most importantly, it happens without the obligatory visit to the store. Your competition isn't the shelf. Your new competition is data, algorithms, near instant gratification and convenience. This isn't the future. This is happening now.

| step two | **Prove your narrative with examples of brands shaking things up.** |

A good narrative description should be reinforced by examples from other brands that prove what's possible and what's coming. These examples should inspire your team by illuminating how far you can go outside of your traditional mindset. The retail space has dozens of great case studies to learn from every month. Learn from the game changers. DTC is a great practice to follow. Here are a few examples of some "classics."

Dollar Shave Club is a classic example of an early adopter brand who ignored the rules of traditional retail, creating a cult following, launching a men's magazine, and growing so quickly that Unilever purchased Dollar Shave Club for $1 billion five years after its launch. Now, it's a brick-and-mortar retailer, too, and still on fire. As we'll see in other examples, click-to-brick is no longer an irony, but a strategy.

Bombas is a success story that attacked a stagnant industry (socks) with a perfect recipe. They have purpose (BOGO for homeless people), a high-quality product (no toe seam), fair pricing (little overhead), convenient distribution (to your door), and a CRM program that has high frequency but is fun (strong brand).

Casper is a young brand disrupting its category with an exciting retail experience. Though it once focused purely on its DTC mattress inventory, it's now giving busybodies in New York the opportunity to take a noontime nap. When you walk into its SoHo pop-up, you're not bombarded with over-eager sales associates and best features for a great price, but instead, the offer of escaping to a nap pod for a midday snooze.

Collect, store and share examples of non-competing brands to inspire strategic vision and new tactical ideas.

---

step three	**Build a customized idea framework.**
	Inspired by the vision and case examples, it's time to build your framework. There are a few key questions to consider. We'll stay with the modern retail model as an example. These types of questions help define an approach for you and your team to consider a new future with retail.

1. What is the consumer benefit of all channels, existing and emerging?
2. Which type of product or purchase cycle is best served through each channel?
3. What value will the channel provide customers and prospects?
4. How is the channel best aligned with your purchase funnel goals?
5. What's coming in social and technology that can help you bypass today's models?

Using the right models will allow you to generate executional ideas that are connected at their core to the principles of all of your concepts: disruption, new forms of utility, partnerships, etc.

The most profound framework is useless if you are not able to generate inspirational ideas that bring your vision to life. This is where you express the brand in new, fresh ways with your communities.

To build a robust framework, assemble a team of outside perspectives; people who do not normally work on your brand. They can come from a variety of disciplines: media, creative, digital, UX, strategy, PR, social business, events. In addition, consider roll-up-the-sleeve work sessions with actual customers. Invite the crazies; as with any work session, success will come from the curation of people with the right attitude rather than people with big titles.

17

Here are some actual ideas that pay off a Rethink the Role of Retail exercise.

Rethink BOGO as BOGS: Buy One Give Something

1-pack, 1-vaccine. In partnership with UNICEF, the 13-year-old campaign has helped protect 100 million women and babies.[3]

THIS SAVES LIVES♥

Snack bars created with the intent of stopping child hunger. Co-founded by Kristen Bell.[4]

The easiest volunteer program on the planet. Each 12-pack purchase restores 500 gallons of river water. Shop to volunteer.[5]

Rethink your Business Model

FOODS

Reduces food waste via direct-to-consumer (DTC) shipments of "ugly fruit." Pantry in a box: This is how to show love to the unlovable while saving a trip to the store.[6]

WARBY PARKER

Disrupted Luxottica, which owned 95% of the eyewear industry previously, to deliver DTC glasses (and trial frames to try on) before moving into brick-and-mortar stores.[7]

Glossier.

Beauty blog-turned-brand that crowdsources consumer intel to directly inform their products. Reviews come to life.[8]

Supreme

Streetwear brand capitalizes on scarcity to hype "drops," recognizing the power of the resale market as a means to exposure.[9]

Rethink your Customer Experience

Athletic wear that encourages customers to put the clothes to practice in-store, with yoga classes offered as stores become studios. Dual-function space.[10]

Functional home decor with a retail space that hosts not showrooms, but your rooms, a guided build-your-own adventure.[11]

Bath + body products; retail space is all about smell and try before you buy — winding, exploratory stores encouraging customers to get hands-on with products as they go.[12]

A fitness franchise that worked around closed locations. When the pandemic struck and gyms were forced to close around the U.S., within a week, Planet Fitness leapt into action by creating "in-home" workouts to help members stay active and healthy while staying at home.[13]

The executions can be endless and the ideas immense. I've seen sessions where we created dozens of great ideas in a two-hour period. The best were then screened and expanded in follow-up sessions with a smaller team, typically 2-3 people who have been charged with idea innovations. The most productive teams include at minimum a media and creative subject matter expert. In general, the fewer team members, the better.

Ask elegant questions

The World Gone Dark brief came from a profound question. Years later, I still use it as a reminder to challenge the creativity of my questions. You should, too. If you are looking to dramatically expand your market share, you need to dramatically expand your questions.

There are dozens of idea spaces for brands to consider, and the list grows new every day. Here are two quick, evergreen areas every brand should question when identifying WGD opportunities: new brand utility and leveraging your culture.

NEW BRAND UTILITY

one   How can you pivot from making people want things to making
           things people want?

_____

_____

_____

_____

_____

two   Can you use packaging or partnerships to entertain and
           inform in new ways?

_____

_____

_____

_____

_____

three   How can you leverage synergy between product utility and your brand story?

four   How can your WGD "media" become a literal translation of your messaging or product?

LEVERAGE YOUR OWN CULTURE

In his forthcoming book, "The Culture Advantage: How to win inside to win outside," strategist and author Jimmy Keown says this on the power of a strong internal workforce in leading a brand to competitive advantage:

"Winning inside is paramount to winning outside and creating a media advantage. It starts with creating a resilient culture and shared mindset that thrives on finding, framing and extracting value for the brand in every possible way. Most importantly, you need a culture that believes in winning for the brand and the consumer, no matter what constraints may exist in media or channel. Sometimes this requires rewriting the rules of media to create and define the media of tomorrow."

---

one   How do you inspire your highest-value segment, your marketing team and employees?

---

two   Can your brand help your employees create a better world for your audiences?

_____

_____

_____

_____

_____

three   What are the ways your organization can make a notable and significant difference, internally and externally?

_____

_____

_____

_____

_____

four   How can you predict and create content that your team would
        be excited to share?

_____

_____

_____

_____

_____

IN SUMMARY - THERE ARE NO SUMMARIES

Just as it's hard to break the rules when there are no rules, it's difficult to have a summary when we live in a world that never concludes.

The smartest marketers know this and take advantage. The truly ground breaking work in communications is driven by imagination inspired by constant change. Your role as a leader is to develop habits that drive imagination and innovation from every corner of your business.

The best leaders know how to ask the right questions of the right people. An innovation structure that works well for me is to schedule daydreams — time to reflect, wonder, research, go down blind alleys, make connections between disparate ideas — to find the right answers. Sometimes it takes some staring out the window as the sun comes up to see things with fresh eyes.

PROMPTS

Are you evaluating non-paid media opportunities, as identified by your audience experts, that can be funded, executed and measured through your media budget?

Have you or can you expand your role to share and integrate audience insights upfront into product development, including packaging, distribution, retail considerations, etc.?

Do you have a modern channel framework using audience insights to inspire and connect ideas from paid, social, PR, digital and measurement teams?

one   Do you have a clear brand purpose that is understood by everyone in your organization?

_____

_____

_____

_____

_____

two   What are the channels at your disposal?

_____

_____

_____

_____

three   Can you find new utility behind the channels?

four   How can you leverage the channels in a way that supports your brand purpose?

five   Do you have the right people involved in developing the ideas?

_____

_____

_____

_____

six   How do you inspire creative problem-solving with your teams?

_____

_____

_____

_____

seven   What are the types of executional examples to drive an emotional connection with your audiences? Do you share these internally?

ON A WORLD GONE DARK, THE TIGER'S CAVE + ELEGANT QUESTIONS

1. nytimes.com/2019/10/28/business/media/advertising-industry-research.html
2. Wikipedia
3. sofii.org/case-study/unicef-and-pampers-1-pack-1-vaccine-partnership
4. thissaveslives.com/pages/your-impact
5. coorsseltzer.com/av?url=https://www.coorsseltzer.com/volunteer
6. imperfectfoods.com/our-mission
7. warbyparker.com
8. wired.co.uk/article/how-to-build-a-brand-glossier
9. indigo9digital.com/blog/the-brilliant-strategy-behind-supremes-success
10. info.lululemon.com/stores/au/brighton/brighton/events/sarahyoga
11. fonolo.com/blog/2019/01/what-ikea-gets-right-about-customer-experience/
12. econsultancy.com/how-lush-is-raising-the-bar-for-in-store-experience/
13. Planet Fitness

TWO

On yesterday's ads, brand new math + bigger ideas

"Nobody counts the number of ads you run;
they just remember the impression you make."

Bill Bernbach

According to a few independent studies, the average American is exposed to between 3,000 and 6,000 advertisements per day, which is what makes this question so fun to ask:

"Do you remember a single ad from yesterday?"

I've asked this question to hundreds of people. The answer is almost always No. No TV, no OOH, no digital ad banner. And worse, I'm typically asking the people who spend 10-12 hours a day thinking, crafting, building, concepting, creating, planning, buying and measuring ads. Some studies also show that 84% of ads go unnoticed, so why even make ads? Can you imagine working in an industry where more than eight out of ten products don't work?

Not remembering ads has nothing to do with passion for the business, or creativity, or how hard people work.

I believe that ultimately, a lot of the blame rests on the distribution of message — media placements that do celebrate the idea.

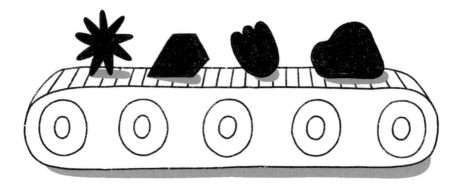

Our business operates like an assembly line. We hand ideas and thoughts and strategies from one department to another, a process that allows a tutti-frutti[14] idea to slowly melt into vanilla. No wonder it's such a challenge to break through the thousands of ad exposures per day.

This, as the world has become even more confusing, with more channels, more social and newer models of communication every week. If we consider the emergence of "paid, traditional" media forms, the touchpoints are vast enough, but if we consider a World Gone Dark definition of media, the touchpoints become cosmic in scale.

"Today you are a channel. You are the medium. You are the message."[15]
Roberto Prado, CEO of NewsPrime

One reason for an entirely new viewpoint on media is that as the influence of media strategy becomes more vital, most traditional media minds still worship at the altar of efficiency and scale. Old myths die hard, but clout and tonnage, with a lot of performance metrics thrown in, do not elevate creativity.

Because of this, most large media agency math has not changed much in the past 20 years:

```
+ + + + + + + + + + + + + + + + + + + + + + + + + + + +
+                                                      +
+   Lower Cost = Media Effectiveness                   +
+                                                      +
+ + + + + + + + + + + + + + + + + + + + + + + + + + + +
```

In other words, for many agencies and brands, a low cost-per-thousand-impressions (CPM) means a job well done. So, you beat upfront cost increases by a few points? You may look good to your client, but what have you lost by winning?

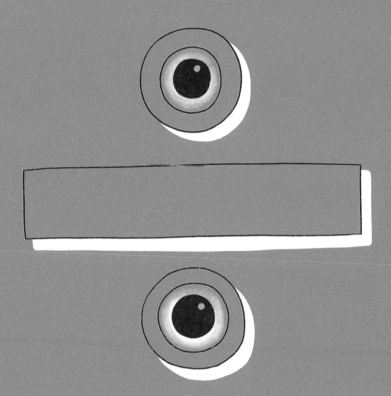

Brand new thinking for strategic media
While some people confuse shiny executional ideas as strategic media, they are not.

Strategic media is a behind-the-scenes art that has been lost in some part due to the explosion of data.

We are still relying on old models of reach curves and optimum frequency levels. But if you dig deeper, the "90% 1+reach" has three forms of contextual media placement:

| one | Context that enhances or becomes the message |

| two | Context that is appropriate but does nothing to add value |

| three | Context that distracts or, as we have discussed, goes entirely unnoticed, perhaps a worse offense |

How do we distinguish the value between the three? The truth is, most clients don't. A client gets a plan, they see they have reach and coverage and they think the media has done its job.

What most brands don't ask is this: is the media schedule stifling the message because the context is not appropriate? How much is just getting the message out? On a media audit, a plan might look fine, but how do you drive up receptivity?

Creativity in media strategy should identify how creative placement helps a brand stand out. This requires a new lens on how we view media.

The purpose of media is to maximize the delivery impact of a brand message to drive business forward. Let's start there.

Recent research provides further evidence of the power of media strategy, particularly placement strategy. In his breakthrough study, "The 360° Advantage: How whole brands dominate," my colleague David Gutting shares a key learning: In persuading an audience, relevant messaging is roughly twice as influential as mass exposure.

This more than calls into question the old orthodoxy of "effective reach" — namely, setting a certain bar for exposure and declaring that to be sufficient for success. There's a better way: fix on the right message in the right context, get it in front of an audience, then eliminate unnecessary exposure and the cost that goes with it.

The study is based on a "relative weights analysis" that determines an influence score for 10 independent variables that determine brand actions in a marketplace. A brand being "seen most often" has 9% influence on total brand value, but "relevant ads/messaging" has 16% influence — second only to "valuable product" at 19%.

The point: sharpen your product value, develop the relevant message and identify high-relevance media delivery opportunities.

Factors impacting total brand value[16]

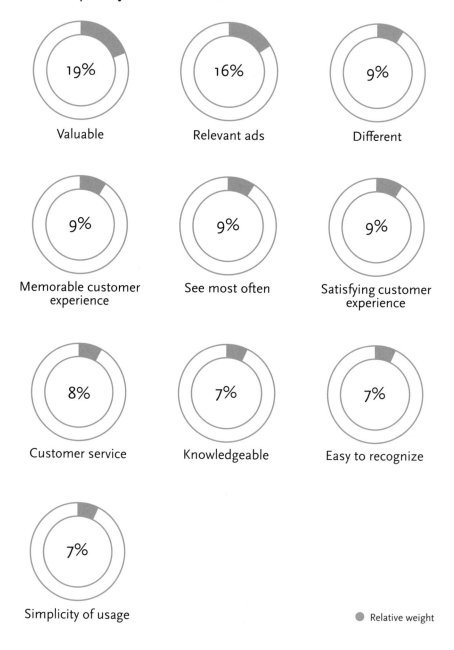

19%	16%	9%
Valuable	Relevant ads	Different
9%	9%	9%
Memorable customer experience	See most often	Satisfying customer experience
8%	7%	7%
Customer service	Knowledgeable	Easy to recognize

7%

Simplicity of usage

● Relative weight

To break from the "efficiency is king" mythology, and to tap into the power of media strategy, we have created a modern media framework that redefines value by harnessing the real impact that media can influence — value that is defined as driving higher impact of the idea rather than securing the lowest cost inventory.

How to Value Modern Media

$$\frac{Idea + Context + Partnerships + Scale}{Cost} = Measured\ Business\ Results\ (ROI)$$

Of course, this is a very basic framework, and should be customized by brand. For some brands, the addition of "flexibility" is critical. For others, the addition of "social influence" becomes critical. But the basic components of Idea, Context, Partnerships and Scale should be considered by all brands.

Modern media considers channel
opportunities that drive the
brand communications back to the
big idea.

Context is Queen

"We need to stop interrupting what people are interested in and be what people are interested in." -Craig Davis

Traditionally, context has meant environment, i.e., surrounding editorial. But message placement should include not only the literal real estate of media consumption, but also as important the frame of mind of the person. This consideration significantly impacts the impact of the message and is why certain premium environments can command a higher cost. But, if you can define your brand's premium environments based on the idea, you can likely avoid typical high-cost inventory. Are your brand high-value moments place-based, moment-based, mindset-based?

A well-crafted customer journey can help influence your priorities, and the best journeys are aligned with the meaning or intent of the idea. The basic components of any journey should include:

- Pathway decision triggers
- Need state
- Channel candidates
- Measurement

Think

Planet Fitness created video and social home work-ins to keep the world moving during quarantine.

Wingstop owned April 20 (4/20) through a one-day blast of binge craving-inspired cable TV viewing with spots that progressively altered the mind throughout the day. Now that's inside baseball.

Reporters Without Borders subverts foreign censorship laws by building a library in Minecraft that houses the "illegal" information.

The Omni-Channel Communications Journey

	Travel Trigger	Research	Decide/Book	Stay	Share	Remind
Need State	Work, Play, Visit	Preference	Location	Safe & Clean	Moments	Joy of Travel
	Experiences	Value	Simplicity	"Gets Me"	Memories	Practical Tips
Vehicles	f, YouTube, CNN, Fox News, Telemundo, Univision, iHeart RADIO, P, hulu, peacock		G, Waze, theTradeDesk	G		Twitter, Instagram, f
KPIs	Branded Search Volume	Segment Conversion	Total Bookings	Mobile Poll	Shares	Open Rate
	Social Engagement	OTA Ratings	Conversion	Grow My6	Sentiment	Conversion
	Direct VS 3rd Party Bookings	SEO Improvements	Speed to Book	Visit Frequency	Positive Reviews	Social Share

Think

The Calm app used a 15-second spot during CNN's highly stressful 2020 election coverage to encourage viewers to do nothing but listen to meditative rainfall.

GEICO created a radio spot that used stereo sound effects to distribute ideas that stimulated left or right brain thoughts of listeners.

Modern media uses context strategically to maximize audience appreciation of the message.

Partnerships

These are the pixie dust of most media investments, where creativity can have significant influence on the effort. Audit your key partner assets to explore areas to engage that are outside of your brand and the media partners' brand typical purview. Perhaps you invest together to create new forms of communication that address your segments' needs. Finding a partner who shares a mindset of "idea value" over "dollar volume" can turn a runner-up media candidate into your most effective partner.

Modern media identifies partners that can provide trust, credibility & content opportunities for the brand.

Think

Progressive Insurance and Whole Foods partnering to provide turkey insurance for Thanksgiving birds.

Volvo partnered with the Sydney Institute of Marine Science to create a living seawall in Australia that directed attention back to its sustainability efforts.

KFC partnered with PentaQ to create Colonel KI, an artificial intelligence commentator who predicts the outcomes of e-sports in China.

Scale

Scale should refer to the delivery of your idea, not your media plan's total reach. Media must consider how your idea can scale through additional weight on primary forms or by inventing new forms of ideas that leverage your media beyond media a la World Gone Dark media.

Modern media maximizes the scale behind the message to break through the noise.

One of the best early examples of the power of rethinking media is the Ice Bucket Challenge. Launched August 2014, this was an activity that involved pouring a bucket of ice water over a person's head, either by another person or self-administered, to promote awareness of the disease ALS and encourage donations to research. It became "viral" with many celebrities, including Bill Gates, Oprah Winfrey, Aaron Rodgers, Lil Wayne, Jimmy Fallon, Taylor Swift, Ryan Seacrest, Demi Lovato, Stephen Spielberg, etc. ALS estimates total donations exceeded $100 million. No paid media.

ON YESTERDAY'S ADS, BRAND NEW MATH + BIGGER IDEAS

View cost as your opportunity, not just what you pay
Paying the lowest price possible is always preferred, but buying exactly what is suited to the idea by leveraging value in non-expected value plays may cost more as a line item but could yield a high multiple on optimal engagement.

Modern media maximizes the value you receive for the investment.

$$\frac{Idea + Context + Partnerships + Scale}{Cost} = Measured\ Business\ Results\ (ROI)$$

Just as no math formula can solve all problems, a modern media framework should take into account your brand climate and needs. What are the other elements that affect how you should plan and prioritize media? Is flexibility critical? Is freshness part of your brand utility? Do you need a context of humor to reinforce brand values? By incorporating purpose, meaning and utility, you can create a math model that will drive higher value from your media investments.

SUMMARY

A new way of looking at your brand's media math opens the lens to a wide range of new value territories, which leads to conversation that opens scopes and drives ideas. Focus on what conditions your brand needs to succeed through the leverage of the media budget, as well as ways to increase the impact of your media investment without increasing your media budget.

PROMPTS

one   How can you use your business model to identify ways to use
        media to affect growth and profitability?

---

two   Have you audited and determined the value of your brand's assets that help determine your math equation?

_____

_____

_____

_____

three   How are you able to estimate and drive value from your existing customer base in your modern media math?

_____

_____

_____

_____

four   What do your customers consider to be the most important brand utility, and how can you deliver that through your media investment?

five   Which elements of the buying process most affect trial, purchase, loyalty, and how can they become implemented in your media investment? (Speed, availability, trust, recognition, etc.)

six   What are the media deliverables that can support your brand
           purpose? (Placement, events, BOGO, etc.)

seven   How can media connect directly to new revenue models?

14. Tutti frutti is a colorful confectionery containing various chopped and usually candied fruits. It is also a song by Little Richard.
15. forbes.com/sites/forbesbusinesscouncil/2020/10/22/yesterday-you-were-just-a-business-today-you-are-a-media-channel/?sh=1b25d1e74c38
16. The 360° Advantage: How whole brands dominate, Barkley®, 2020. wholebrandproject.com

THREE

On the art of haiku, a miserable failure + flywheels

"To convey one's mood
In seventeen syllables
Is very diffic— "

John Cooper Clarke

I once led a global strategy team of a few dozen people spread across the world. These were quite brilliant people, each quirky and unique in their own personal and cultural way.

My job was to create a language of sorts, a system for us to work with, to generate insights. Much of our work involved heavy lifting of research to find the "nuggets" of information that would become inspiring insights.

We tried a few methods and we had a process flow, which was pretty similar to all of our competitors' approach. Because of this, I would constantly push for ways to think, explore and contemplate in unusual ways, to try to break our minds free of standard methodologies, but to also infuse a "flavor" or "sound" for our team to unite around. Something to make us special. And of course to have some fun.

One method that turned out to be a miserable failure was to try to distill insights and ideas into haikus. This was valiantly attempted a few times. It forced us to focus, but didn't result in better ideas.

To start a habit,
Four weeks. Twice a day. Habit formed!
You're hooked. Listerine!

Such limitations can spur creativity, but sometimes the box is just a little too confining. We quickly dropped the notion of using haiku as our form of communication inspiration.

But my fascination with distillation is perhaps one reason I love the flywheel.

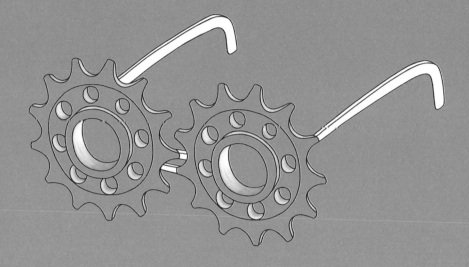

A flywheel is a mechanical device specifically designed to efficiently store rotational energy (kinetic energy). Flywheels resist changes in rotational speed by their moment of inertia. The amount of energy stored in a flywheel is proportional to the square of its rotational speed and its mass.[17]

I find flywheels are business art. Similar to haiku, it is the ultimate form of business elegance. It instantly communicates the intention of the business and the role of every constituent, identifies opportunities and drives revenue, efficiently.

The flywheel concept originally gained fame in Jim Collins' book "Good to Great," but it was the Amazon flywheel that brought widespread attention to the immense power of a well-constructed flywheel.

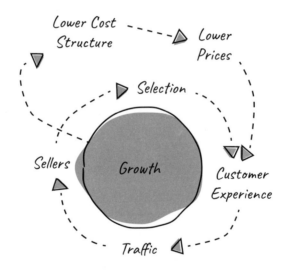

The real power of the Amazon flywheel is that it requires no explanation. Whether you are Jeff Bezos or a receptionist in Rufus, you know the dynamics that drive the Amazon business.

Also, as a business model, flywheels are never stagnant but evolve to stay true to the core business competency. The Amazon flywheel grew to look like this:

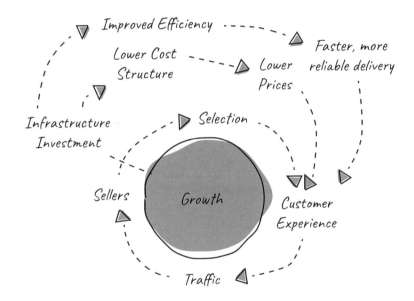

So how does this apply to media? If you agree the concept of Brand New Math equates to modern media as we laid out in the previous chapter, you realize the power of value extraction from every dollar invested and recognize "non-obvious" values of media partners and ideas. Given the media budget is typically an organization's largest single line-item investment, using a flywheel approach to that investment makes sense for several reasons:

---

one | Media can be an overly complicated discipline; a flywheel provides clarity, focus to and priorities when building media strategies.

---

two | A well-constructed flywheel can unlock investment connections and opportunities with media partners.

---

three | A flywheel is useful when sharing rationale behind complex, large media investments to teams/CEO/Boards.

---

four | The mere act of building a flywheel with the right team members drives collaboration and creativity.

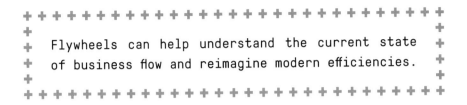

Flywheels can help understand the current state of business flow and reimagine modern efficiencies.

The United Way is one of the first global nonprofits, built for good in 1887. Today, the brand is experiencing troubles operating in a new world of technology, social impact, speed of ideas, and fierce competition. The rules and behaviors of giving have changed as dramatically as any industry over the past several years.

It's no wonder that UW donations are trending down; in fact, between 2007 and 2017, United Way saw charitable donations decline 27.9%.[18]

United Way's current state is a large organization focused on two things: finding people willing to donate money and helping local organizations. The more money donated, the more good for the local community. It looks something like this:

United Way Today

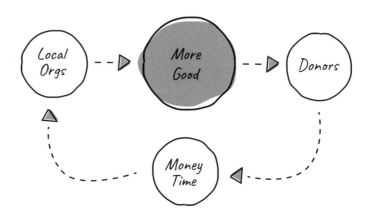

United Way Future State

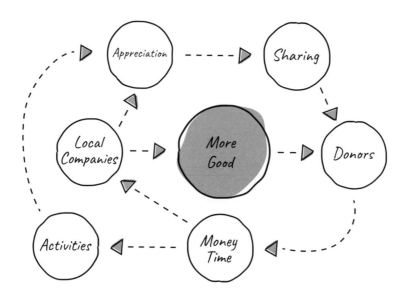

But given everything we know about modern culture, about millennials and Gen Z need states, about technologies, about social habits of sharing and getting credit for good, the old UW model does not live up to modern expectations.

We worked with a key UW local chapter to explore a new model that addressed modern charitable giving.

The new model featured the elements/ingredients that are critical to success, driven by a need for appreciation. This can take many forms, mass or personalized, but appreciation has the dual value of both reinforcing good donation behaviors and becoming a shareable opportunity. Donors want to do good and they want to get credit for doing good.

Flywheels: the Swiss Army knife of team alignment.

One form of value of a flywheel exercise is the mere act of having the conversation. What is in the center? What are we trying to achieve as an organization? How do we identify and connect the drivers that will impact our success? These discussions help drive the business needs forward, but as importantly, they align teams on mission and purpose.

By applying the right constructs and flow to a well-articulated flywheel, you can focus your team on vital points of responsibility and deliverables in a clear, simplified manner. The efficiencies work to manage teams and partners to drive cohesiveness and quality of bigger ideas.

But the real beauty of the flywheel is that it can be applied to any number of business goals: volume growth, share growth, efficiency growth, innovation growth, and of course, greater media efficiencies.

From a practical perspective, most brands have several external partners, with blurred discipline responsibilities — paid media, digital media, social, creative, CRM, SEO, PR, and in some cases, multiple local media buying teams. The goal of all team members is to drive media investment effectiveness, but the roles can become muddled as turfs overlap and agencies compete for revenue. A concise flywheel approach can develop clear roles and swim lanes, while pushing each agency to maximize output of their deliverables.

Let's take a quick look at a retail business with local and national media agency partners. At its simplest form, it reminds everyone of the drivers to maximize media spend and efficiency but showing the desired evolution of attracting customers.

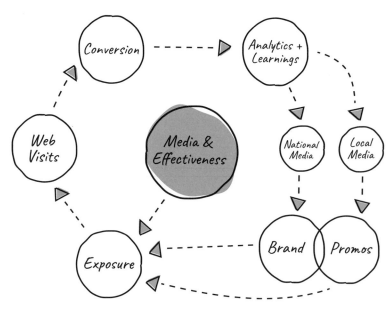

In addition to basic understanding of how the business operates, this flywheel provides a lens through which all agencies can connect ideas and add value by asking and applying data and insights from other areas.

As the flywheel spins, it continually reveals optimizations that leverage and grow the center, in this case, investment effectiveness.

It is a business haiku.

Spin, flywheel, lev'rage
investment effectiveness
Continually!

This is just the beginning for the work that a flywheel can do.

Here are a few additions to the same flywheel that begin to enhance media effectiveness. Again, this is an organization that relies on several agency partners, and collaboration and synergy are the key drivers to business success. Redundancy and wasted energy are the drags to higher business performance. This level of additional clarity solves for the drags.

Capitalize on every touchpoint, no matter the journey

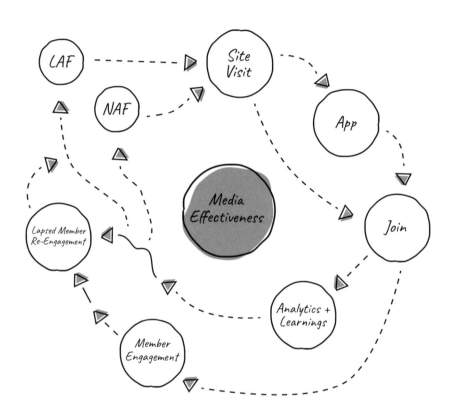

Local Media (LAF): Brand- Digital Market-Warming | Promo (Required, Local and Flash)

National Media (NAF): Brand- TV Market-Warming | National Promo

Local and National Media Task Awareness
- Video (National & Spot TV, OTT, OLV)
- Display
- Audio
- Partnerships
- Social (Organic & Paid)

Lapsed Member Task Reengagement
- Email
- Social (Paid)
- Display
- SEM

Site Visit Task Consideration
- Display
- Social
- OLV
- SEM
- Partnerships

App Task Prospect Engagement
- Social (Organic)
- App Content

Join Task Conversion
- SEM
- Email
- In-club Experience

Analytics & Learnings/Member Engagement Task Brand Love & Loyalty
- App
- Social (Organic & Paid)
- Email
- In-club Experience
- Partnerships Pull-Through

The orbits around this goal are aligned to represent the influence of media with a very defined goal of web visits. Media is charged with awareness to drive web traffic. Seems simple enough. But it's what happens to that web traffic (conversion) and how we understand why things are happening (analytics) that begin to create spin for the flywheel.

There is a tendency for brands and agencies to share massive dumps of "learnings," without thoughtful consideration for who needs to know what, when and how, resulting in dozens or sometimes hundreds of wasted hours for an organization. Using a flywheel helps to ensure that subject matter expert (SME) constituencies receive specific actionable insights. Streamlining and editing the analytics bubble can improve quality, speed and appropriateness of knowledge share.

SUMMARY

The benefits of a media flywheel mentality spread beyond roles and goals. It can define the relationships between media companies and brands. This is where the investment traction literally hits the road.

As you develop a media flywheel expertise, imagine and design modern methods of framing up desirable outcomes between brands and media vehicles by highlighting and focusing ideas, energies and dollars into the spaces that drive the highest impact.

A well-articulated media flywheel is your future. It simplifies your extremely complicated business landscape by allowing you to design efficient, easily communicated business models, create new forms of thinking and identify new skill sets that can help your brand develop an extremely strategic media team.

PROMPTS

---

one · What are you trying to grow with your media — customer base, distribution, margin, new segments, new ideas, efficiencies?

two   What are the core drivers of growth — scale, distribution, segment insights, efficiencies?

three   How do the core drivers impact the business growth objective?

four How can you align resources to maximize the spin?

_____

_____

_____

_____

five What is the proper order of the impact of influence —
new resources, financial, partners, realignment,
communications, etc?

_____

_____

_____

_____

17. en.wikipedia.org/wiki/Flywheel
18. Charity Watch

FOUR

On urgency, creative generalists + flow

"A good idea for a new business tends not to occur in isolation, and often the window of opportunity is very small. So speed is of the essence."

Richard Branson

"I feel the need, the need for speed."

Maverick

FOUR

Big ideas can come from anyone, but whole brand communications is a team sport.

"Consider professional basketball, hockey and soccer teams. They don't just measure goals; they also track assists. Organizations should do the same, using tools such as network analysis, peer-recognition programs and value-added performance metrics."[19]

But as you optimize the speed of ideas, it is as important to identify waste. Wasted time and energy is the supervillain to great work. The world moves faster than ever, with levels of integration and globalization never imagined. Technology is the key driver, but "human" workflow is the real opportunity for organizations to succeed in this new world.

Speeds kills (your competition).

According to a recent Boston Consulting Group (BCG) study, ad agencies spend up to 80% of their time on non-value-creating activities. I think the same could be said for most corporate marketing departments.

Many agencies spend significant time on non-value-creating activities [20]

Agency activity analysis shows on average one day of value-creating activities in five days of campaign process time.[21]

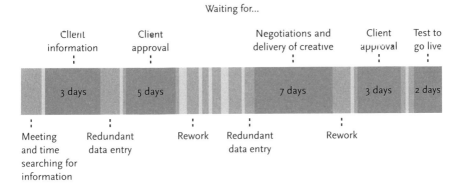

Time to "go live": 25 days

Planning	Activation		
	Search Setup	Reservation	RTB

Waiting for...

Client information	Client approval		Negotiations and delivery of creative		Client approval	Test to go live
3 days	5 days		7 days		3 days	2 days

Meeting and time searching for information | Redundant data entry | Rework | Redundant data entry | Rework

● No activity on that specific campaign | 20 days
◐ Non-value-creating activities | 4 days
○ Value-creating activities | 1 day

83

Why? Things like silos, poor system integration, approval bottlenecks and redundancies can take a toll on productivity. But the real loss is not losing efficiency, it's the opportunity cost of not driving faster, bigger ideas.

Your org structure and workflow is likely one of the most complicated tasks to manage in the world. This is particularly true in the field of marketing, which has high turnover, rapid consumer change, almost daily technological advancements, and delivers a product that makes emotional connections with people. No, we are not saving lives, but we are investing millions to earn billions. If you want to get grandiose, we drive the world economy.

Speed and integration win.

Building a culture of speed and integration is essential for several reasons. What follows are not reasons it's hard but reasons to do it anyway:

one	Your customers expect it.
two	The faster you move, the more you learn.
three	Marketing should lead your organizations.
four	If you don't integrate with speed, your competitors will.

If your brand is not evolving, your future is bleak. Marketing textbooks are littered with logos from the graveyard: Blockbuster. Toys "R" Us. AOL. Compaq. Borders Books — and very soon, other large antiquated models including a few airlines, universities and, gulp, ad agencies.

Modern companies use workflow/process as a competitive advantage, and this is no truer than in the communications business. Workflow is the most underrated and powerful tool to inspire and drive your organization. If you are not reevaluating your systems process every year, and fine-tuning it more frequently than that, you are not optimized.

To determine how necessary a workflow update (or overhaul) is to your organization: Are you doing things the same way as you were doing things two years ago?

+ +
+   +
+   To determine how necessary a workflow update (or   +
+   overhaul) is to your organization: Are you doing   +
+   things the same way as you were doing things one   +
+   year ago?   +
+   +
+ +

Here is a quick checklist to see how vulnerable you are to a world of change. If you find any of these issues impeding the development of your marketing communications, it's probably time to take a fresh look at how you build your brands.

◯ Do your business briefs define a business problem that lead to a communications solution?

◯ Can you define roles, inputs and outputs for every discipline in your team?

◯ Can your organization define what great work looks like?

◯ Does your internal comms approach provide collaboration and structure that shows in your product?

◯ Are your big ideas more hypothesis-based than data-led?

◯ Is "comms planning" relatively unknown or too complicated for your organization?

O   Do you have a disciplined and consistent customer journey in place?

O   Is there productive collaboration between your creative and media agencies?

O   Does it take longer than a few days to get an idea in-market?

O   Do your agency partners have unique tools that essentially do the same thing?

O   Does last year's media flowchart look the same as this year's flowchart?

Long live the creative generalist
Tim Galles, author of "Scratch: How to build a potent modern brand from the inside out."

The main output of an efficient marketing process is to share timely relevant insights to inspire great work. As with most decision-making, it must be considered, thorough and fast.

Where to begin
As with most business opportunities, a quick needs assessment can help to establish your brand's goals and challenges. Start with a clear goal and challenge. Here is an example:

Corporation X goal
To develop and implement an integrated communications planning approach across all brands. Approach must be grounded in integrated insights, lead to a strong communications idea and be executed in a way that expresses the brand idea in the market.

Corporation X challenge
The brand works with multiple outside agencies and several internal marketing teams and manages several brands ranging from $100K to $1B+ in sales. Our way of working should reflect an ability for all key stakeholders to understand and value the role and responsibilities of every team member and their output.

Corporation X brand culture
After setting goals and defining challenges, developing a set of core beliefs is crucial to focusing on defined ideal outcomes. This is driven largely by the overall corporate philosophy and should be developed quickly, within a few days. Think about it like this: If purpose is the why of your brand, beliefs are the how — the operating instructions. Let your beliefs guide everything your brand does, inside and out. Try to make these actionable, observable, assessable, trainable, and rewardable. Make certain they align with the customer experience you want to deliver. Need a jumpstart? Take a look at your founder's history, mission statements, annual reports, web experience, employee interviews, your best customers, social feeds.

Seven guiding philosophies to building the perfect workflow

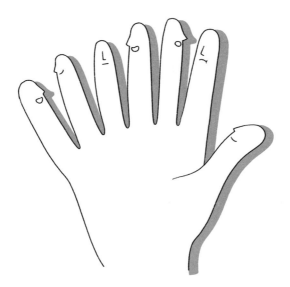

1. Simplicity
The simpler, the better. Building a communication plan is already complicated without having a complicated workflow. Give people a very clear understanding of their role.

2. Consistency
For the sake of efficiency, brands need a system that is consistent with their values and categories. As a side benefit, consistency will drive institutional knowledge for career management.

3. Flexibility
We need to understand that the needs of each brand may differ based on scale, complexity, marketing conditions, changing cultural habits, etc. Organizations need a way of working that provides essential work points with potential pivots to shift energies and focus when necessary.

4. Inclusion
All agencies, departments and team members must provide value, and more importantly, feel valued, but only at the appropriate time. It is important to understand workflow connections between the right groups as well as larger touchpoints to share knowledge, get consensus and build community.

5. Data infused
Data should drive decision-making, not paralysis. Relevant data points increase confidence and speed-to-market. But, data should be viewed as a workhorse, not a show pony. Data that does not impact sales or growth is distracting. Become a data minimalist.

6. P&L mentality
Every single person on your team should understand the basic tenets of how and where the brand makes money. They should also know exactly how they contribute, with measurable goals aligned either directly or indirectly to profitability.

7. Celebration
Laissez les bons temps rouler. Organizations are defined by what they celebrate, so says Jimmy Keown, author of "The Culture Advantage: How to win inside to win outside." People want to be recognized for good work. Celebrating actions that are important to the organization helps define behaviors and drive commitment.

A well-developed and integrated communications planning approach across all brands will not only streamline better work, but also train your workforce for growth by understanding a customized approach to brand development.

Ideally, the approach should consider employees as influencers who are engaged through a shared purpose, aligned with our vision and values, and think brand in everything they do.

What are your impediments to growth?
Your workflow should acknowledge the marketing failures and opportunities of your category. All organizations have nuanced rules and ways of working that help optimize ideas. All also have impediments. In our work with large organizations, we find most brands need to move from:

Disconnected ⟶	Connected communications
Closed ⟶	Open systems
Fixed ⟶	Fluid work process
Risk ⟶	Opportunity-minded
Consumer fixation ⟶	Understanding communities through shared values

Words matters

As simple as it sounds, it is critical to identify "value-creating" focus and actions by establishing a common language. Here are examples of very simple language that must be understood by everyone on the team. These terms are very basic, but the real value comes from clearly defining the unique language and colloquialisms of your organization. Every company has its own unique shorthand. Sharpen it.

key terms	Simple descriptions that inform value of contributions
owner	Responsible for the product/idea development
leader	Responsible for approval, feedback, course correction
stakeholders	Responsible for feedback and integration of ideas
inputs	Tools and resources to enhance product or ideas
outputs	Insights and outcomes that drive idea enhancement

What does innovation mean in your company? What is a big idea? What must be considered and included in a media recommendation? Ask ten people and you are likely to get nine answers. In addition to developing a dictionary of expectations and responsibilities, develop a common language around precise meanings of terms used within the organization. Some examples:

big idea	A single sentence that describes an emotional, distinct, shareable and universal idea that breaks through culture
journey	Identifies, defines and prioritizes key brand opportunities to connect with the right communities at the right time, place and mood
comms strategy	Roadmap that inspires creative and media ideas to connect the big idea with the audience
creative execution	Concepts, production and real-time management of messaging
media execution	Plan containing investment summary of media strategies, ideas, partners, timing and costs
innovation	Unexpected ideas that expand beyond modern expectations

The work flow

Building an integrated, productive workflow is essentially building a puzzle, except in most corporations, all of the puzzle pieces are squares so the puzzle can be arranged in a number of ways.

Still, every marketing plan requires a few basic ingredients: a business goal, a marketing goal, customer and prospect insights, strategies, tactics, ideas, executional rigor and a measurement plan.

To build a customized platform requires a focused commitment to drive the process from the intersection of the product and audience.

What is paramount is that the process is easily understood by everyone engaged in the marketing communications process. We are in the communications business after all.

We have found great success by distilling the entire system framework to a large placemat. This forces elegance by including only the very necessary elements in a flow that use input from the prior step and add value to the next.

The following example illustrates virtually everything you need to know to develop strategically superior work for a modern brand. This includes all the requisite information for a brand marketer to operate successfully.

The Master Comms Process features only the absolutely necessary element. The workflow outlines the steps and insights necessary to build ideas that incorporate all tools (journey, comms idea, comms framework).

Communications Planning Overview

What do we need to be successful?
Develop and implement an integrated communications planning approach across all brands to affect 2021 and beyond. In addition, it is critical to ...

As a general principle, move from:
1. AAA to BBB resources
2. CCC to DDD systems
3. EEE to FFF process
4. GGG to HHH constituents
5. III to JJJ communities

Current State:
• Comms planning is ...
• Briefs are ...
• No consistent AAA in place
• Brand briefs should be ...
• Lack of clear ...
• Overwhelming amount ...

Current Needs:
• Develop comms model to ...
• Define role and deliverables ...
• Define role and cadence of ...
• Prioritize simplicity while ...
• Must provide ...

Why is this important?
The world has changed and conventional communications models have not kept pace. There is an opportunity to develop a customized communications planning model that is custom to XXX based on a consumer-focused, data-led, approach to ideas and channels that connect our brands with communities in a modern, simple, collaborative way.

1 Master Communications Process

Priority Segments
• Strategic Audience
• Current Users
• Media Target
• Competitive Target

• What is the state of my business?
• Who is growing/declining my business?
• How do buyers relate to my business/ what else are they buying?
• Who drives my business?
• Where do they spend their time?

Partner Operating Principles
• "Big picture" sessions
• Consistent, scheduled feedback
• Clear and enforced roles

4a Responsibility of the Communications Framework

Blends Brand Brief, Audience Deep Dive (+CDJ), the Big Idea and Moments into a Communications Delivery Framework (CDF).

• Inspires the mechanics of all executions
• Amplifies the big idea for creative
• Defines barriers and tasks
• Should inspire ideas, channels, technology and owned media in new ways

Leads to high-value creative media partnerships and ideas by leveraging the power of uniting message and delivery through a data-led, consumer lens.

2a Category Decision Journey Framework

See It	Want It	Buy It	Share It
Media Social POP	Media Social POP	Work Home On-The-Go	WOM Social In-Person
When and where do they see it? What touchpoints are the current and future consumers using?	What retailers are buyers going to vs strategic target?	Where is purchase occuring and with whom?	Where, when and why to share and are they an influencer?

We see an opportunity to blend category framework with specific brand research.

2b Decision Journey

Message / Triggers & Timing / Notes & Goals / Desired Outcome / Comms Touchpoints

Trigger → Trigger → Trigger → Trigger

3 Communications Idea

Brand Ambition / Brand Purpose / Core Beliefs / True Believers / Red Thread / Positioning / Promise / Editorial Authority / Voice

4b Communications Framework

True Believer / Insight / Communications Strategic Idea / Creative Partnerships

In addition to creating a flow to produce work, it is as necessary to define responsibilities, timelines and language. The back of the placemat is useful for sharing details of operational structure.

Communications Planning Overview

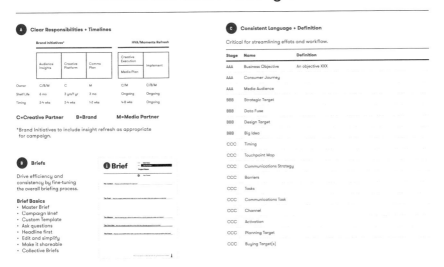

This should be customized based on the idiosyncrasies of the industry and brand. The point is that there is freedom and room to capture everything that will provide more efficiency and connectivity between agencies, departments, teams and ideas.

This framework is a vital tool in reimagining your communications planning for a world gone dark. Download an editable version at commsplan.barkleymedia.us.

What does this yield for large companies? We've seen:

one	Uncovering redundant resources to find savings of hundreds of thousands of dollars.
two	Reducing the timeframe of "idea to on-air" from months to days.
three	Ideas so integrated that it is impossible to tell where it began: Was it a media idea or a creative idea or a brand idea or a research idea?
four	A highly functioning team that understood the swim lanes to deliver higher value.

And what is the financial impact of these advantages? Hard to measure the impact on sales but easy to find numerous studies on stock price, share growth and brand value of highly functioning organizations.

Optimizing workflow should be a fast-moving process to capitalize on a changing world. A period of three months is normally sufficient time to explore and develop a modern solution. The process should consider at minimum the following inputs:

Internal and external audit (4 weeks)
Interview key stakeholders
Identify need states of partners
Audit partner agency tools
ID global best practices

Explore (2-4 weeks)
Identify best practice tools
Find gaps in tools and talent
Integrate brand positioning
Create custom customer journey
Develop streamlined process
Determine needed resources

Implement (4-6 weeks)
Develop and rapid test framework with 1 3 brand leads
Manage process and workflow
Recap value of tools/stages/flow

Iterate (ongoing)
Automate
Constant evolution
Best practice sharing
External audits

SUMMARY

How long have you been operating in your current state?
Have you seen your dentist in the past year? Have you changed the oil in your car in the past six months? When was the last time you reevaluated your workflow?

The fastest way to build powerhouse brands is to modernize the way that your organization builds powerhouse brands. Keeping pace with changing technologies, multiple audiences' need states, a constantly changing culture, competitive pressures from everywhere and macro effects on the global economy all demand that you have a finely turned operational process. If you have not audited how you work in the past 12 months, you are not optimized.

PROMPTS

one   When was the last time you evaluated your workflow
       and process?

two   Does your framework drive efficiency to maximize idea output to drive growth? What can you stop doing?

_____

_____

_____

_____

three   Are you incorporating modern tools and a framework that provides full alignment of your teams?

_____

_____

_____

_____

four   Have you included the right data and measurement tools to continually optimize your model?

five   Have you created the right conditions for your teams to succeed?

six   Do you have a system to audit and learn from competitors outside your category?

19. HBR Collaborative Overload Jan 16. https://hbr.org/2016/01/collaborative-overload
20. BCG- Cutting Complexity 5/13
21. Process time represents the total time spent actively working on the campaign and excludes waiting time.

FIVE

FIVE

On the mass age, the power of creativity + special guests

"The linearity of the text in an average book wouldn't do.
After all, the medium was the message!"

Quentin Fiore

You may remember that book by Marshall McLuhan "The Medium Is the Massage," the one that predicted global villages and people riding waves of information. Publication year: 1967. "Massage" was a printer's error, but McLuhan, a wordsmith who delighted in puns, liked the typo and kept it, believing that it amplified his theory about how different forms of media thoroughly "massage" the senses in the "mass age" of communications. Clever.

The book was merely philosophy and prediction until it came across the desk of one quirky designer by the name of Quentin Fiore — who wanted to literally build McLuhan's ideas into the book's pages. Some pages were printed backward, to be read in a mirror. Some of the writing was upside down. Some pages contained text superimposed over pictures. The result was the first interactive/interconnected book of the information age.

This is media creativity as its finest.

```
+ + + + + + + + + + + + + + + + + + + + + + + + + + + + + + +
+                                                           +
+   It is your responsibility to improve the power of       +
+   creativity in media.                                    +
+                                                           +
+ + + + + + + + + + + + + + + + + + + + + + + + + + + + + + +
```

Ideas drive every aspect of our business. We are an idea business. And the case for creativity has been made over and over again. We study creativity, we award creativity. It is the well-spring that drives our industry and business growth. It is fun. It is daunting. It is fulfilling. It is maddening.

Creativity is within every single one of us. Whether you love or hate an ad, you have a POV on creativity. We are all experts on some level.

Media is no different, but I would argue media is a tougher space to be considered creative. There are many reasons for this:

The Discipline
The work product of media can be very transactional and a primary role is investment advisor.

The Talent
Media typically draws upon math-oriented people, meaning they are more likely to be linear and logical.

The Deliverables
Media is often looked at as an executional practice. It is hard to be creative when your core product is a flowchart.

The Expectations
Media people are often not expected to produce creative ideas.

So imagine a world where we could overcome these challenges to inspire media talent with the expectation that their ideas could change the creative reputation of the entire media discipline. Imagine the enormous value by driving higher standards of creative media ideas through creative media executions.

"Judge a man by his questions rather than by his answers."
Voltaire

Q. How do I help you think about media creativity in a new way?

A. I get by with a little help from my friends.

So that's what I've done. I've asked some of the smartest people in the business that work WITH media, about creating great work.

The questions are simple but get to the heart of ways to view media through a creative lens.

one	How do you stay creative?
two	What is media?
three	What makes a media idea creative?
four	What makes a creative media person?

(Writer's note to all my friends: This was the most difficult chapter to edit because of the dozens of provocative, philosophical responses from many of you. If you did not make the book, know that you made my mind. Thank you.)

Lachlan Williams
HEAD OF STRATEGY, RGA LONDON

How do you do creativity?
As much as possible.

I look for the tension between stuff. I smash different things that I find interesting together in different ways and combinations with different people to see what jumps out. I look at a problem from as many angles as I can, and then throw a bunch of ideas onto Post-its, paper, whiteboards, voice memos, shared docs or whatever is closest. I go over it again and again until stories begin to emerge.

What is your view of media?
Having started my career in media, I've always felt it was both undervalued and underutilized in the creative process. I see it as simultaneously the context in which culture is formed and shared as well as the means to connect at scale. It should be central in how an idea should manifest. But it's not about what comes first, media or creative. It should be creativity first, and media / message should happen in whatever order makes sense. But ideally, together, with no separation.

Lastly, it's folly to think that ideas travel without proper investment in media. That doesn't mean you have to buy media in a traditional way. But there is no such thing as free anymore. You pay for amplification, no matter the context, no matter the platform.

What makes a media idea creative?
It just has to be a good idea to begin with, ignore the media bit. I like to replace the word media with context.

```
+ + + + + + + + + + + + + + + + + + + + + + + + + + + + +
+                                                       +
+    Forget about the baggage that comes with the idea  +
+    of a platform, a sales tool or media-buying. And   +
+    just think about how context inspires creative     +
+    solutions. The best media ideas understand and     +
+    activate context in a creative way.                +
+                                                       +
+ + + + + + + + + + + + + + + + + + + + + + + + + + + + +
```

What are the traits of the most creative media person you know?
The unique ability to simultaneously think in an abstract, conceptual and dynamic way AND then switch to a detailed, focused, executional and technical way. Great contextual creative thinkers understand the substance of culture and the infrastructure. They can stretch across both the concept, execution and experience — building creative ideas that travel well beyond the initial thought and add value to people's lives and the brand across the whole ecosystem.

Anything else?

If media agencies want to exist in a world where the trading of media space can be automated or taken in-house (which is coming very, very fast). Then they need to find a way to optimize their offering based on creativity, not commission. Great media thinkers are hard to come by, but they are a critical piece (and an often missing one) for the building of modern brands.

Lastly, this will be the year that businesses and brands are forced to adopt digital. And they are going to need help. Who better to do that than the experts in context and format. Step up, media-folk.

Matt Maher

FOUNDER, M7 INNOVATIONS

How do you do creativity?

I start with defining what creativity is: the act of bringing something new into the world. It can be something actual, like a piece of art or music, or it can be intangible, like an idea, thought or new way to solve a problem. Regardless of its form, creativity is the catalyst that triggers an emotion. It is the qualitative, the gut feeling, the unique output that never quite has a linear path from its conception to its unveiling.

I take the approach of reverse engineering creativity. I often imagine a desired outcome, then think of the best paths to get me there. Often, it's in this journey to this desired result that the destination shifts, or I find myself going down a completely different path. Whatever that final outcome may be, it's the amalgamation of experience and subjective problem-solving that got me there. Therefore, creativity is a sum of its parts and paths chosen, it can be neither right, nor wrong, it is merely a reflection of its creator.

What is your view of media?

Media is everything. Media is everywhere. The IMAX movie screen in front of you. The smartphone you just silenced. The clothing on every person in the theater around you. The slightly accented chair you are sitting in. The oversized cup you just picked up. The scent of AMC-style butter that permeates from the bag. Every physical thing that exists in our world was created purposely, and its message lies in the eyes of the beholder. Media, then, is an assault on our senses, and humans are skilled at leaving most of it outside the gaze of our perception. Only the most forward-thinking marketing minds can use media to stimulate these senses and create a resonating impact.

What makes a media idea creative?

I refer back to Marshall McLuhan's quote from 1964, "the medium is the message." In order to make a media idea truly creative, you have to both masterfully navigate the expectations of the specific medium, but also be willing to break a few unconscious rules to make an impact. Today, with media consumption increasing while attention spans decrease, creativity in media requires you to pleasantly disrupt a user's expected experience and puncture their autopilot. Today's media consumption consists of endless scrolling on Instagram, 10-hour binges on Netflix and trillions of texts sent via messaging platforms. Creative media ideas need to stop the scroll in its tracks, pause the stream and make users go from type and send to copy and share.

What would you recommend a media person do to become more creative? We, as humans, have been using tools for millions of years. From stone-carved pots of the Paleolithic era to the Excel-built pivot tables of the Digital Era, tools help humans in forming their inputs and gets us to our desired outputs. For a media person, take stock of all the tools you use every day, then categorize them as quantitative or qualitative. Which tools take your binary input to get your desired output? You won't find much creativity there. Which tools require thought, problem-solving and a subjective input to get to your desired output? Those are the qualitative tools that will force you to flex a creative muscle in your brain you may not be used to using. If you have no tools you use in the latter category, discover them and start a trial. The internet enables us to be as autodidactic as we're willing to be.

Lastly, take Isaac Newton's quote to heart. "If I have seen further than others, it is by standing upon the shoulders of giants." Absorb all of the amazing work that has taken place in the media world over the past 20, 50 or even 100 years. Learn from the best, soak up that creative output and use it to refuel your creative input, bringing something fresh into the world.

Matt Seiler

**HEAD OF RAINES
INTERNATIONAL'S MARKETING &
COMMUNICATIONS PRACTICE**

How do you do creativity?

Creativity starts with a brief. There's an Ogilvy line I bastardize, which is something like "God grant me the freedom of a tight creative brief." Creative is just luck if it doesn't start with a reason for being. Something on which it is based. Something against which it can be measured.

What is your view of media?

Somewhere along the way, we lost the meaning of media. Today it is just another name for math. Numbers. Delivery. Media is so much more than that. It is the medium. Literally and figuratively. A canvas if you will. As a great old spot buyer once said to me of his role ..."without me, they (ads) are just home movies!"

What makes a media idea creative?

You can't really have one without the other. Media or creative. Creative by definition has to take some form, and media is that form.

+ +
+   +
+   What makes a media idea creative, and what makes   +
+   a creative idea a media success is the marriage   +
+   of message with medium — something where we are   +
+   better off for having been a part of the messaging.   +
+   +
+ +

I think about two of my absolute favorite ads, both out of home, and recognize that had I heard them, or read them in a magazine, they would not be on the top of my list. Guinness: "Only 100 calories. Not on Purpose." Schwab: "Wow. I am 50!"

What are the traits of the most creative media person you know?
Boundless curiosity. A refusal to accept medium or message. Or medium versus message I suppose. One who really lives, and can imagine or even embody the people who will interact with the messaging.

What did I miss?
This is fun.

SARAH IVEY
CEO, FOUNDER AGENTS OF NECESSITY

How do you do creativity?
I have started to work in two modes these days – one that uses a bag of tricks, techniques and prompts, and another that's more meditative and iterative (and maddening). It's kind of like Edison and Tesla. Edison relied on a team of people using standard techniques to get to reliable responses – that's the kind of reliable creativity that I get from the bag of tricks. The Tesla method (which isn't a method at all) relies on chewing at a problem over a longer period of time – kind of like thinking that the creative solution is out there if only you can hear it/tune into it. I work on it a bit, do something else, sleep on it, come back at it and do a lot of dreaming. This is the only way I can get to deeper insight work that leads to better creative solutions.

What is media to you?
The lines blurred quite some time ago so that it's difficult to separate the "medium" from the platform from the content from the utility. Media planning I think has become far less about the channel/selection/rationale etc. – nearly every media plan has the same elements. This is such a positive thing — I think we're seeing the rise of the next generation of media craft. Media has many dimensions now: channel, platform, context, content, behavior, utility, so that the potential for creativity I think has actually increased.

What makes a media idea creative?

Well, I think a great creative idea these days has to have a brilliant media component to it anyway, and the very best ideas are so well integrated that you can't see the join between creative, content and media. In other words, it's a great media idea that stands on its own as a strong idea full stop.

Think about the most creative person in media you know: what qualities or abilities do you think make them so good at what they do? One of the qualities I've observed about really gifted innovators in media is that they speak in ideas, all the time – it's like a tap they can't turn off. I think the sheer volume of ideas is, in itself, a bit of a habit. It's getting out from under the perception that you have this one miraculous idea that comes down from the clouds of Olympus. It's getting into the habit of throwing many ideas up on the wall, and keeping it going. One of them will be a winner. And in that volume, there's also a bit of detachment.

```
+ + + + + + + + + + + + + + + + + + + + + + + + + + + + + + +
+                                                           +
+   Great ideas, when they're finally executed, are the     +
+   work of many iterations and many hands, and to get      +
+   the ideas to that point, you have to see how they       +
+   could be improved while still sticking to the core      +
+   idea, and that means letting the idea have a life        +
+   of its own.                                             +
+                                                           +
+ + + + + + + + + + + + + + + + + + + + + + + + + + + + + + +
```

Tom Demetriou
EVP / CREATIVE, BARKLEY

How do you do creativity?

As I get older, I recognize I cheat by going back to patterns of thinking that have worked for me in the past. It's like chess. There are basic patterns and if you have them memorized, you can use your brain on other considerations. But I always have to be careful to try to throw all that away at some point in the process and be a child, think from scratch, etc.

The shift in creativity for me now is shifting my old training: creativity is what a writer and an art director come up with -> creativity is what new / interesting / different partners we bring in when we've found the idea and need to bring it to life in a way that's native to channels.

What is media to you?

Media is the way people see/ hear / encounter our idea. It could be a prank. A dance party. A plug on a podcast. I think of experiences like The Museum of Ice Cream or Meow Wolf. They're their own mediums, aren't they? They're also wildly appealing photo ops for people's own social media channels, so that's part of their genius and relevance (in a pre- or post-Covid world). I still make the old mistake of thinking about media as a one-way channel, TV first, etc. — bad habits. But I think that's OK. People only want to interact with a brand so much. People only want to do so much math, or none. We still want a show. Netflix is king because it lets you veg out. So putting the story out there for people, if it's a good enough story, to just passively consume and enjoy is still a valid approach. Sorry, you asked about media. Maybe there's an answer in there somewhere!

What makes a media idea creative?
Short answer would be context and timing. Lowe's puts out a ton of helpful video content on YouTube. It's fucking terrible. Doesn't matter. It contains highly desired content. I guess at least 6 million people want to know how to make walkway pavers — God bless them. That's the best way for people to access it. Self serve meets them where they're at. That doesn't really answer your question, but it gets at it. It wasn't creative but it's totally right. I'd value right over novel. But I'd value novel + right over everything.

What would you recommend a media person do to become more creative?
Oh man. I dunno. There's the annoying yet true advice to just be more observant about the world. Watch what people watch. What makes people look? What gets ignored? I'm always amazed every year during the Super Bowl there's always one quiet spot (in recent years Google) that makes the whole Super Bowl party room stop and look because, duh, silence is actually arresting in the context of all that noisy shit everybody else is pumping out. Be familiar with channels and how people actually use them. But always be a student of human nature.

FINAL

FINAL

On a World Gone Light, morality and media + David Bowie

"The path of least resistance is rarely the path of wisdom."

Tim Cook

THOUGHTS

This last part is pretty important.
It's about the impact of you.

In the marketing world, customers vote with their pocketbooks. It follows then, that advertisers vote with their budgets. Our industry, with billions in our pocketbooks, may have the world's greatest impact on truth — and with that morality.

Seismic change comes from people, not institutions. Think Greta Thunberg and Tim Cook. If brands find profit from good, isn't the highest good a strong sense of morality? If so, the people who manage big brands (that's you) have a gift and an obligation to the world, to be personally responsible. It is at the core of being a good human.

—

Next, a startling confession: We have allowed disinformation.

The news networks are our doing.
The social networks are our doing.
Privacy, ad fraud, lack of transparency are our doing.

Mistrust is partially our doing. Maybe more than partially.

We have the power to make the world a better place. I, you, we, control a lot of money. Billions and billions of dollars that can impact our world. We invest in traditional media and World Gone Light media, and those investments can make the world a better place. Or not. It's our choice.

I'll say it again, we control ALL the money.

Whether you are inspired by Steve Jobs, Cindy Gallop or David Bowie, there has never been a more critical time to be big and bold and brave. The movement has begun. To sit on the sidelines would be a tragic waste.

As we move into a period of redefining or reinventing or even a total dismantling of our industry, take with that a sense of empowerment of the difference you can make.

What if we see every action, every investment, through a lens of good?

Don't fund systems that mislead.
Don't fund media that distribute lies.
Don't fund bad people.

If a few people with pooled, small investment budgets can successfully attack Wall Street institutions, just imagine what our creative minds can accomplish to do good.

Thank you for listening. Thank you more for doing.

"The future is very important. Don't wait for it. We make the future as we make the truth." -D. Bowie.

BTW: Add Good has been an operating principle for me these past several years. If you are interested in staying aware of my thoughts on this topic, text me: 816-389-7178, or go to: letstalk.barkleymedia.us.

Jen Mazi
I always wanted a muse, and when I think of you, I am reminded of that classic line, "How can you take someone from crayons to perfume?" You did just that. You took a bunch of scribbles, fragments and complete randomness and stirred it together to make something special. Thank you.

Tim Galles
When I met Tim at Keens Steakhouse in Manhattan on a particularly stormy day, I knew in an instant that I had met my extended mind. I have never had an uninteresting conversation with you.

Jeff King and Dan Fromm
You are my friends, co-workers, leaders and bosses. Thank you for pushing me to do this. I am adding mentors to the list.

Hannah Lee, Joni Thomas and Arthur Cherry
You added elegance, thoughtfulness and whimsy to this book in the most beautiful unexpected way. I cannot thank you enough for bringing these concepts to life.

Barkley Media Team
How do you put up with me? You are the kindest, hardest-working, most honest and earnest team of people I've ever worked with. You make it so much fun to explore our world. You inspire me every day.

Bear
You sat at my feet, showing love and support, throughout all the mornings and nights, as I pieced this book together. Your slobber drives me crazy, but you are a best friend.

✚ The Advantage Series

Each book in this series works in tandem to help you find competitive advantages that lead to growth and opportunity in a market that's changing by the minute.

✚ The Purpose Advantage:
How to unlock new ways of doing business
By Jeff Fromm + Pip Cross | 2019 + 2021

From eye-opening interviews with some of the world's most successful CEOs to a step-by-step workshop, this breakthrough book is the ultimate guide for turning your brand's purpose into a competitive advantage.

✚ The Culture Advantage
How to win inside to win outside
By Jimmy Keown | Coming Soon

The most successful strategies, ideas and visions are achieved when your internal culture adopts them across the organization. Achieving such consensus and inside commitment means winning hearts, minds and decisions internally — key to creating whole brands.

Cross, Philippa, and Jeff Fromm. *The Purpose Advantage: How to Unlock New Ways of Doing Business*. Vicara Books, 2021.

Cross, Rob; Reb Rebele, and Adam Grant. "Collaborative Overload" Harvard Business Review, January-February 2016. hbr.org/2016/01/collaborative-overload

Galles, Tim. *Scratch: How to Build a Potent Modern Brand From the Inside Out*. Kansas City, MO.: Barkley, 2020.

Field, Dominic; Olaf Rehse; Kristi Rogers, and Paul Zwillenberg. "Cutting Complexity, Adding Value: Efficiency and Effectiveness in Digital Advertising." Boston Consulting Group, 2013.

Gilliland, Nikki. "How Lush is Raising the Bar for In-Store Experience." Econsulancy, Jan. 26, 2018. econsultancy.com/how-lush-is-raising-the-bar-for-in-store-experience

Gutting, David. "The 360° Advantage: How Whole Brands Dominate." Barkley, 2020. wholebrandproject.com.

Hsu, Tiffany. "The Advertising Industry Has a Problem: People Hate Ads." New York Times, Oct. 28, 2019. nytimes.com/2019/10/28/business/media/advertising-industry-research.html

Keown, Jimmy. *The Culture Advantage: How to Win Inside to Win Outside*. Kansas City, MO.: Barkley, 2022.

McKinnon, Tricia. "The Brilliant Strategy Behind Supreme's Success." Indigo Digital, May 28, 2019. indigo9digital.com/blog/the-brilliant-strategy-behind-supremes-success

McLuhan, Marshall, and Quentin Fiore. *The Medium is the Massage*. Bantam Books, 1967.

Mehra, Samantha. "What IKEA Gets Right About Customer Experience." Fonolo. fonolo.com/blog/2019/01/what-ikea-gets-right-about-customer-experience

Prado, Roberto. "Yesterday You Were Just a Business; Today You Are a Media Channel." Forbes, Oct. 22, 2020. forbes.com/sites/forbesbusinesscouncil/2020/10/22/yesterday-you-were-just-a-business-today-you-are-a-media-channel/?sh=1b25d1e74c38

Turk, Victoria. "How Glossier Turned Itself into a Billion-Dollar Beauty Brand." Wired, Feb. 6, 2020. wired.co.uk/article/how-to-build-a-brand-glossier

A

B

C

G

H

I

J

K

W

Barkley is an independent creative idea company committed to knowing modern consumers better than anyone in order to build whole brands from the inside out.

barkleyus.com | wholebrandproject.com

Jim Elms

Jim Elms is the Chief Engagement Officer at Barkley — a "rare find in the world of media agencies!" his colleagues exclaim. He's worked at W+K, Goodby, Grey, UM, Initiative, and IPG Corporate in a variety of roles including head of global strategy, chairman, and IPG managing director. Most recently, Elms served as the Global CEO of Initiative where he was responsible for $15 billion in media, managed a global team of 2,500 people in 80 countries. During his career, Jim has managed relationships with Got Milk?, Nike, Unilever, Anheuser Busch, and created the Rufus network — IPG's bespoke global Amazon agency.

In 2014, Jim was named Media Executive of the Year by Media Magazine. Pretty much every year before and since, those who work with him call him an inspiration.